池田晃久
AKIHISA IKEDA

I just realized that with this volume, this manga is in its second year! To all you readers—thank you! Creating literature is the result of "passion." As for myself, thanks to the inner fire of "I want to draw!" I've kept going all this time! All right, it's only been two years, but still... Maybe it's because I have energy to spare, but this volume's story might have gotten a little intense... Once in a while, please humor me when I do stuff like this, okay? *[laugh]*

Akihisa Ikeda was born in 1977 in Miyazaki. He debuted as a mangaka with the four-volume magical warrior fantasy series *Kiruto* in 1999, which was serialized in *Monthly Shonen Jump*. *Rosario+Vampire* debuted in *Monthly Shonen Jump* in March of 2002, and is continuing in the new magazine *Jump Square* (Jump SQ). In Japan, *Rosario+Vampire* is also available as a drama CD. In 2008, the story was released as an anime.

Ikeda has been a huge fan of vampires and monsters since he was a little kid.

He says one of the perks of being a manga artist is being able to go for walks during the day when everybody else is stuck in the office.

ROSARIO+VAMPIRE 6

SHONEN JUMP ADVANCED Manga Edition

STORY & ART BY AKIHISA IKEDA

Translation/Kaori Inoue
English Adaptation/Gerard Jones
Touch-up Art & Lettering/Stephen Dutro
Cover Design/Ronnie Casson
Interior Design/ Ronnie Casson
Editor/Annette Roman

ROSARIO TO VAMPIRE © 2004 by Akihisa Ikeda
All rights reserved. First published in Japan in 2004 by SHUEISHA Inc., Tokyo. English translation rights arranged by SHUEISHA Inc.

The rights of the author(s) of the work(s) in this publication to be so identified have been asserted in accordance with the Copyright, Designs and Patents Act 1988. A CIP catalogue record for this book is available from the British Library.

The stories, characters and incidents mentioned in this publication are entirely fictional.

No portion of this book may be reproduced or transmitted in any form or by any means without written permission from the copyright holders.

Printed in the U.S.A.

Published by VIZ Media, LLC
P.O. Box 77010
San Francisco, CA 94107

10 9 8 7 6 5 4 3
First printing, April 2009
Third printing, September 2011

www.viz.com

www.shonenjump.com

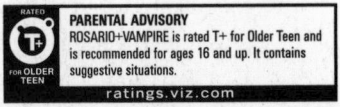

Rosario + Vampire

Ghouls

6

Story & Art by

Akihisa Ikeda

The Horror Story Thus Far
Through a bizarre series of events, Tsukune Aono finds himself enrolled in Yokai Academy—a private school for monsters! When Moka Akashiya, the most beautiful girl in the school, wants to be his friend, Tsukune is determined to stay...despite the school rule that any humans who learn of Yokai's existence must be slain!
After joining the Newspaper Club with Moka, Tsukune's life is blissful...except for being attacked by the school "Enforcers" and battling a witch in the human world over summer vacation. Moka must save his life repeatedly by infusing him with her blood, turning him temporarily into a vampire.
As the 2nd quarter of school begins, Tsukune is elected class president, stalked by an abominable snowgirl, and attacked by a jealous gang of "monstrels." Once again he survives through an infusion of Moka's blood...but at what cost...?!
Moka Akashiya
The school beauty. Turns into a vampire when the cross on her throat is taken off. Tsukune is her favorite classmate...and Tsukune's blood is her favorite food!
Tsukune Aono
The lone human at Yokai Academy, and the only one who can take off Moka's rosario. With Moka's blood in his veins, his strength is equal to that of a vampire.

Yukari Sendo
An 11-year-old witch who likes Tsukune and Moka. Although smart enough to skip several grades, she's still as impish as any preteen.
Kurumu Kurono
A rather obsessive succubus who has settled on Tsukune as her "Mate of Fate."
Ruby
A witch and disciple of the Lady of the Knoll. Ruby hated humans until she experienced Tsukune's kindness. Hospitalized at the moment due to injuries sustained in battle.
Kusabi Mido
A "monstrel" who views all purebred monsters as his enemy...and thinks Tsukune is one of them.
Mizore Shirayuki
An abominable snowgirl able to manipulate ice. She missed most of the first quarter at Yokai Academy, but fell in love with Tsukune after reading his newspaper articles.

CONTENTS

Volume 6: Ghouls

Test 21 Bad Blood 7

Test 22 A Kiss 52

Test 23 Ghoul 93

Test 24 Nightmare 135

21: Bad Blood

DM M
WAK
THUKK
...

YOU ORGANIZED MEMBERS OF OUR GANG TO ATTACK TSUKUNE AONO, DIDN'T YOU?
YOU DIS-OBEYED MIDO'S DIRECT ORDERS!
UHH ...

NO YOU DON'T, SAIZO! YOU'RE NOT GONNA PASS OUT ON ME!
YKK

KRAK
THUD
GUH
KKRK
KK

W
K

SHAK
AND THEN YOU GOT YOUR ASS BEAT... LOSER!
GUH!
WMP
KSSHH
SEE, THIS IS WHAT I HATE ABOUT MONSTRELS ...
YOU NEVER KNOW IF YOU'VE GOT ONE WITH REAL TALENT OR JUST MORE TRASH.
HO
HO
I TOLD YOU—WE DON'T FORGIVE LOSING.
PLEASE ...
F-FORGIVE ME... MIDO...
PL...
PLEASE ...
WHK

MONSTERS WHO POSSESS POWER NO PUREBRED WILL EVER HAVE...
DIAMONDS SCATTERED IN A PILE OF GRAVEL...
...AND THE OTHER KIND... THE ONES WHO DON'T DESERVE TO LIVE.
LIKE YOU, SAIZO.
NO...
HEH
YEAH. LIKE YOU.
GRP

HARDLY, IDIOT.
MIDO... YOU MEAN... YOU'RE GOING TO COVER FOR THAT PIECE OF—
THERE'S JUST...
NO NEED TO TELL THE HIGHER-UPS ABOUT THIS YET, IS THERE?
!
FWP
NO! PLEASE
GAH!
DM
WK
WD
THD
...SOMETHING I'VE GOT TO DO FIRST...
...SLAY TSUKUNE AONO!!

HOOOOO
AAAH!
TSUKUNE ?!
WHAT HAPPENED ?!
ARE YOU HURT?! YOU'RE ALL BANDAGED UP!
HUH...?

OH, THESE?
FORGET IT, KURUMU. IT'S NOTHING.
AHEM
HA HA HA
BUT... BUT...
I JUST GOT JUMPED BY SOME MONSTRELS YESTERDAY.
DON'T KNOW WHY. THEY JUST...WENT AFTER ME FOR SOME REASON!
BUT I'M FINE.
REALLY?! BUT...YOUR NECK...IT LOOKS...
OH, THIS?
NAH, THIS ISN'T FROM THAT FIGHT!
...?
!
PINCH
THERE'S NOTHING TO WORRY ABOUT. REALLY!
...
TSUKUNE...

THIS IS A BIG DEAL ...
IT'S NO BIG DEAL...
YEAH... BUT MOKA'S BLOOD TURNED ME INTO A VAMPIRE FOR A WHILE SO...
HUH ...?
UHH

YOU WENT UP AGAINST THE MONSTRELS, TSUKUNE?
...MONSTRELS ?
OH!

DOOOM
PLUS, THEY'VE FORMED A GANG. MAKING ENEMIES OUT OF THEM ISN'T GOOD FOR YOUR HEALTH.
THE THING ABOUT MONSTRELS IS THAT THERE ARE SO MANY OF THEM.

...
YOU NEED TO BE REALLY CAREFUL. THEY'RE BOUND TO RETALIATE.
BRRR
THIS GANG OF BAD-ASS MONSTRELS CONSIDER ANY PUREBRED AS THE ENEMY.
ES-PECIALLY LATELY, I HEAR...
PUREBRED
MONGREL
PUREBRED

DID SOMETHING ELSE HAPPEN TO TSUKUNE?
MOKA... ARE YOU HIDING SOME-THING?
"WHAT HAP-PENED" ...?
!
S-SO... HOW DO WE STOP THEM?
I NEVER WANT... WHAT HAPPENED... TO HAPPEN AGAIN!
!
GULP
HA HA
YOU BETTER TELL ME!
IF YOU'RE HIDING ANYTHING, I'M GONNA BE SOOO MAD AT YOU!
KURUMU ...?

FOMP
'CAUSE IF ANYTHING BAD HAPPENS TO HIM...
I'D NEVER FORGIVE MYSELF!
WAGH?!
BUMP
GOOSH

PEEK
...

OW! OW!

...
YEEOW!
WHAT'S WRONG ?!
M-MY INJURIES... AND YOUR CHEST...!
GOOSH

SCRIBBLE
I MISSED SEEING TSUKUNE FIGHT.
SO THAT'S WHAT HAPPENED YESTERDAY.
TOO BAD...

READ THIS WAY
TELL ME THE TRUTH...
UM... TSUKUNE ?
YOUR NECK...
IT HASN'T REALLY HEALED, HAS IT?
THE WOUND FROM WHEN I...INFUSED YOU WITH MY BLOOD...
...
HUH?
OOPS
...
...
NO, NO! IT'S TOTALLY HEALED!
REALLY!
WHAT A LOUSY LIAR...
HAHAHA!
GEEN
FWIP FWAP

I MEAN...
!
IF IT HAPPENS AGAIN...
...WHAT AM I SUPPOSED TO TELL KURUMU AND EVERYBODY?
COME ON! BE HONEST WITH ME!
BING
...THIS WEIRD TRANSFORMATION, RIGHT?
...YOUR BODY TO UNDERGO...
...IT'S MY BLOOD IN YOUR VEINS THAT'S CAUSING...

!
SURE, I FELT A LITTLE FUNNY YESTERDAY, BUT I'M FINE TODAY!
TH... THAT'S R-RIDICU-LOUS!
HA HA HA
SHUDDER
"TRANS... FORMA-TION"?!
GULP

TAKE THAT BANDAGE OFF YOUR NECK...
IF YOU'RE SO FINE— SHOW ME!

STOP! DON'T PULL!
WAK! MOKA?!
LET ME SEE!
MOKA!
RRR RRR
WOW P

URK!
PSH
...AND LET ME SEE!

I DON'T HAVE TO SHOW YOU ANYTHING!
!
...
...
HF
HF
HF
HF
HF
HF
HF
...
AND IT'S NONE OF YOUR BUSINESS!
IT'S IN MY BODY NOW!
IT DOESN'T MATTER IF IT'S YOUR BLOOD!

TSU-KUNE ...?
TS...
WSH
HARD TO BELIEVE, MIDO...
IS HE REALLY A SUPER-STRONG VAMPIRE?
SCRAWN-IER THAN I EX-PECTED.
HMF.
SO THAT'S TSUKUNE AONO...
THP

HEH
HEH HEH
THE BLAZING RED EYES...
HIS BRUTE STRENGTH ...
YOU'LL BELIEVE IT WHEN YOU SEE IT WITH YOUR OWN EYES...

SNEERING DOWN AT US WITH THEIR FANCY PRIVILEGE...
THE ELITE OF THE DAMNED PURE-BREDS!
AND WHAT A TROPHY— A VAMPIRE!
...WITH THE BLOOD OF ONE OF THEIR OWN.
I'M GOING TO TAKE THEM ALL DOWN A PEG...
...LURE THE VAMPIRE TO ME.
OF COURSE. BUT FIRST, I NEED TO...
SERIOUSLY? YOU'RE REALLY GONNA DO IT...?
BDMP

BRING ME THE BAIT.
BRING ME... HER.

PLEASE...
SIGH
TINK
TELL ME...
WILL HE RECOVER...?
WITHOUT MY HELP...
...WILL TSUKUNE'S BODY BECOME...
...
TINNN
NNNG
HEY! I KNOW YOU'RE UPSET, BUT— HEADS UP!
PIP
YOU'RE IN DANGER!
WHAT...?
TOOM

VSH

HO O OOOOO
NEXT DAY...

AND WITHOUT LETTING ANYONE KNOW...
MOKA'S USUALLY SO ON TOP OF SCHOOL STUFF...
HM...

HUH? SHE ISN'T HERE?
THAT'S NOT LIKE HER...

HEY!
YADA YADA

I DIDN'T MEAN TO UPSET HER. I JUST DIDN'T WANT HER TO WORRY ABOUT...
HMM
IS THIS BECAUSE OF OUR FIGHT YESTERDAY ...?
SOME-THING WRONG?
GOING
ACK!! N-N-NO!! NOTHING!!
MNCH MNCH MNCH
...?
WELL, SHOOT... THERE WAS SOMETHING I WANTED TO TALK TO MOKA ABOUT...
WHAT ?
ABOUT...THE MONSTRELS WE WERE TALKING ABOUT YESTERDAY.
I GOT KIND OF WORRIED SO I ASKED GIN ABOUT THEM...
AND HE SAID...
YOU WANT TO KNOW ABOUT THE "MONSTRELS" ?

...RIGHT. MONSTRELS. STEER CLEAR OF THEM.
!
POW
STOP THAT!
MISH
GOOSH
WELL, NOW.. LET ME THINK...
Hmmm
...FORMED A GANG TO GRIND EACH OTHER'S AXES.
EVEN THE ENFORCERS ARE AFRAID OF THEM.
STARE
MONSTRELS ARE EGOTISTICAL. THEY HATE LOSING MORE THAN ANYTHING.
SOME OF THE MOST POWERFUL ONES HAVE BANDED TOGETHER AND...
?!
I WAS GOING TO WARN MOKA...
I WANT TO MAKE SURE WE'RE *ALL* ON THE LOOKOUT FOR THEM.
REALLY.
GOOSH
I'D HATE TO SEE YOU GET HURT...
...
...

TSUKUNE ...?

PFFF

TINGLE

SHUDDER

YEEP ?!!

...

You don't have to run away...

?!

SHH

VWISS

BRRR

KU-KU-KURUMU?!

WHISH WHISH

!

HEY, TSUKUNE...

DID SOME-THING HAPPEN BETWEEN YOU AND MOKA?

HUH?!

JOLT

I CAN TELL. YOUR HEAD'S A MILLION MILES AWAY.

AND YESTERDAY MOKA ACTED LIKE SHE WAS HIDING SOMETHING.

I KNEW IT.

DOES MOKA...
...HAVE SOMETHING TO DO WITH...
...THIS WOUND OF YOURS?
BOOM
W-WOUND?
I'LL BE MORE SPECIFIC.
DID MOKA CAUSE THAT WOUND, BY ANY CHANCE?
BDMP BDMP
UH...
Female Intuition
IF SHE DID...
...I WILL NEVER EVER, EVER FORGIVE HER!
I HOPE YOU KNOW, TSUKUNE...
SOB...
...THAT I WOULD NEVER DO ANYTHING TO HURT YOU!
BDMP

I'D RATHER DIE THAN HURT YOU!
!
UHH... OF COURSE!
HUH?
THANKS, KURUMU!
Kiss Op
BOMP
HEY!
TSUKUNE! WHERE ARE YOU GOING?!
VSSH
?!!
...
STUPID ...
GRR

WHY DIDN'T I SEE IT...?
IF I'M GOING THROUGH SOME WEIRD TRANSFORMATION...

MOKA MUST THINK IT'S BECAUSE OF HER BLOOD!
SHE'S BLAMING HERSELF FOR WHATEVER'S HAPPENING TO ME!
I'M SO STUPID! HOW COULD I SAY SOMETHING SO AWFUL TO HER WHEN SHE WAS ALREADY HURTING?

IT'S NONE OF YOUR BUSINESS!
I'M JUST AN IDIOT, THAT'S ALL.
I'VE GOT TO APOLO-GIZE TO HER!
YO!
WHERE ARE YOU RUSHING OFF TO, TSUKUNE AONO?
TMP
!

PERHAPS YOU'RE...
...LOOKING FOR SOME-ONE?
TM

WHAT ...?!
TOO OO
OOOM
?!!
SO THE REASON SHE WASN'T IN SCHOOL TODAY...
!!
THAT'S... MOKA'S BAG!
...
YOU WON'T FIND WHAT YOU'RE LOOKING FOR IN HER DORM ROOM...
WHIF
?!
!
IF YOU WANT HER BACK... COME WITH US.
?
THAT SHOULD TELL YOU MY BUSINESS WITH YOU...
WE HAVE MOKA AKASHIYA.
MY NAME'S MIDO. I'M A MONSTREL.

HOOOOO

SHEER

NO! DON'T COME HERE, TSUKUNE!

TSUKUNE ?!
IF I GET KILLED, NO ONE WOULD EVER KNOW...
?!!!

NO ONE COULD HEAR ME CALL FOR HELP...
THAT'S BAD...
THE ABANDONED SCHOOL BUILDING...?

GET AWAY! HURRY!
MOKA!
...
GASP
SH
VSH

COME, NOW...AFTER ALL THE TROUBLE WE TOOK TO KIDNAP YOUR GIRL, DO YOU REALLY THINK WE'D HAND HER OVER SO EASILY?
IF YOU WANT HER BACK, YOU'LL NEED TO TAKE HER BY FORCE!
COME ON... VAMPIRE.
NNK...
SHH
TSUKUNE !
DM
DM
DM
GUH ...
KSSSH
HAAAAK

V... VAM...
VAMPIRE?! ME?!
OH!
SHH
HOOO
I HATE GUYS LIKE YOU.
RICH LITTLE BRATS FROM YOUR PURE BLOOD-LINES.
BWK
MRK
THINK YOU'RE SO FUNNY CALLING US "MONSTRELS," DO YOU?
MMMG
KKKK
HOOO

WELL, IT'S TIME FOR US MONSTRELS TO SHOW YOU...
...WHO'S REALLY TOP DOG.
KOOM
DM
VSSH
TM TM
TM
TK TK
TK
TAKA TAKA

I COULDN'T EVEN SEE HIS ATTACK! HE'S...
WHAT... POWER ...!
H OO
O O
TAK TAK
HWOOO
OOOO

HO
BOOM
MWK
WK

TM
TM
HSSH
GULP
BRRRR
COME ON! TAKE IT OR BLOCK IT!
SHHWP
BWK
BWK
I'M NOT HOLDING BACK ON THE NEXT BLOW, VAMPIRE!
OO
SHP
SHP
HOOO
BAMP
BAMP
BAMP
BAMP

STOP!
YOU'RE MAKING A MISTAKE!
?!!
HE'S NOT THE VAMPIRE YOU WANT!
I AM.
?!
WHAT ...?
THIS WHOLE MESS IS ALL MY FAULT.
TSUKUNE'S TRANS-FORMATION, HIS SUFFERING, HIS PAIN...
I'M TO BLAME.
SO IF YOU WANT TO HURT SOME-BODY...
...HURT ME.

YEAH... NOW THAT YOU MENTION IT...
TMP...
SOB SOB
!
!
SAIZO SAID SOMETHING LIKE THAT...
NO...
MWG
!
HOW CAN I BLAME YOU FOR ANYTHING ?
RGH!
YOU'RE THE REASON I'M ALIVE!
YOU'VE GOT TO BELIEVE ME, MOKA...
MOKA! YOU KNOW THAT'S NOT TRUE!
HOW CAN THIS BE YOUR FAULT?

YOU'RE THE BEST THING THAT'S EVER HAPPENED TO ME!
SSSS
SHH

FL
...COMING AT ME HEAD-ON?!
SSSSH
WHAT DO YOU THINK YOU'RE DOING...
MK MK
SSSSH
I GUESS THE BOY REALLY WANTS TO DIE FOR YOU, VAMPIRE!!

?!!
ZSH

?!!
...
IMP...
H-HEY...
HOW DID HE...?
?!
TS... TSUKUNE ...
WOBBLE
SSS
NNNH...
SSSSSSS
WHAT ?!
TSUKUNE !!
TSU-KUNE ?!
WMP
HF
MWK MWK
HF HF

MOKA... YOU'VE GOT TO BELIEVE ME...
GASP!
NN
...
NN NN
NO MATTER WHAT... I'LL ALWAYS BE GRATEFUL TO YOU.
TING...
WSH
KIIIIIIN
TIK TIK
TMM
WHAT ARE YOU DOING ...?
WHY AREN'T YOU ATTACKING ?!

KK
DON'T ACT LIKE I'M NOT EVEN HERE!
GWP...
MWP MK VRRP
CHNK
THP

?!!!
YOU DARE RAISE A HAND AGAINST ME?
PIECE OF TRASH...
KNOW YOUR PLACE.
CLNK
SHAK
SSSSHHHH
DMMMH

READ THIS WAY
WHAT ...?
BUT... THERE'S A LOT YOU DON'T UNDER-STAND.
TMP
IT EASED MY HEART A LITTLE.
HW
WHAT YOU JUST SAID...
TSU-KUNE ...
TNK
I GUESS THIS IS AS GOOD A TIME AS ANY...
DO YOU REALLY WANT TO KNOW, TSUKUNE ...?
ABOUT YOUR WOUND? WHAT'S GOING TO HAPPEN TO YOUR BODY?
HOO
TNK
BDMP
BDMP
GULP...
I-I...
BDMP

22 : A Kiss

WELL?
WK

SHALL I TELL YOU ABOUT MY BLOOD, TSUKUNE ?
WHAT TOO MUCH OF IT IS DOING TO YOUR BODY?
ABOUT THE TERRIBLE DANGER YOU'RE IN RIGHT NOW?

DOOO
OOOOM

MOKA ...?
!
NOBODY BEATS MIDO WITH ONE BLOW!! HE'S INVINCIBLE ...
IMPOS-SIBLE!!
HOOOO
SNAP
WSH
HEY ...
NO WAY !!

YOUR BODY... IT'S STARTING TO BREAK DOWN.
IF I INFUSE YOU WITH ANY MORE BLOOD... IT'LL PROBABLY KILL YOU.
THAT'S HOW FRAGILE YOU ARE.

SS...

HEAR ME OUT, TSUKUNE...
!

AM I... DYING?!
"BREAK DOWN"? WHAT DOES THAT MEAN?!
PLIP

PLIP
EEP!

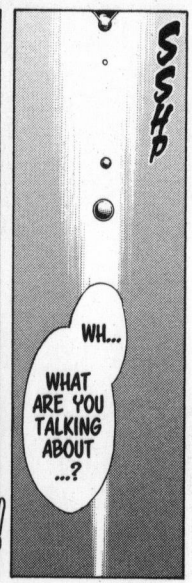
SSHP
WH...
WHAT ARE YOU TALKING ABOUT ...?

IT ISN'T HOPE-LESS.
YOU STILL HAVE A CHANCE... IF YOU RETURN TO THE HUMAN WORLD RIGHT AWAY.
THAT WOULD GIVE YOUR BODY A CHANCE TO HEAL ITSELF.
BUT...YOU WON'T BE ABLE TO COME BACK TO YOKAI ACADEMY.
WHAT ...?!

YOU CAN'T EVER HAVE ANYTHING TO DO WITH THE WORLD OF MONSTERS AGAIN!
?!

BECAUSE THEN... I'LL NEVER BE ABLE TO...
...SEE YOU AGAIN ...
YES. I KNOW.
HA HA HA
?!!

WH-WHAT ARE YOU TALKING ABOUT?
YOU'RE JOKING, RIGHT?
CHINK

HOOO

BUT IT ISN'T ME YOU'LL MISS, IS IT...? IT'S THE "NORMAL" MOKA!
WE BOTH KNOW THE TRUTH.
WHATEVER HAPPENS BETWEEN YOU TWO HAS NOTHING TO DO WITH ME!
WE'LL NEVER SEE EACH OTHER AGAIN...?
NOTHING TO DO WITH...?
DO I REALLY MEAN THAT LITTLE TO HER?!
KRIIK
KRI
CHK...

?!!
SHE DOESN'T CARE IF I GO...?
IDIOTS.
IDIOTS.
BLABBING IN THE MIDDLE OF A FIGHT!
VSH
VSH
VSH

HEH... THIS IS PAYBACK FOR THAT LITTLE KICK...
SSH
HOOOOOOO
BWK BK
...VAMPIRE!!!

WKKK

STAY BACK, TSUKUNE!
KRAK
M...
MOKA!
TMM
IDIOT!
SSS

RRO OOM!
DID YOU...
...HEAR SOME-THING? LIKE A... RUMBLE?
A RUM-BLE?
OVER THERE...
HUH...? KURUMU?
?
IRK!
HEY! BAZOOKA GIRL!
HEY!
!
I DON'T WANT TO BE NEGATIVE, BUT...I'VE GOT A BAD FEELING ABOUT THIS...
?

C-CAN WE TALK?

FRIENDS?!

I THOUGHT, SINCE YOU TWO ARE FRIENDS...

BRRR

...

...

THIS IS AN EMERGENCY.

!!!

I DON'T HAVE TIME TO ARGUE WITH YOU...

RING

SHE WAS STALKING HIM! RUN HER OFF!

SCREECH

And who you calling friends?!

And who you calling friends?!

HEY!

YOU'RE THAT ABOMINABLE SNOWGIRL WHO WAS CHASING AFTER TSUKUNE!

TSUKUNE'S BEEN KIDNAPPED— BY THE MONSTRELS!
YOU'VE GOT TO HELP ME SAVE HIM!
PLINK
Ngh!
HUH?!
S-SORRY...
BUT I CAN'T DO IT ALONE...
THERE ARE TOO MANY OF THEM... AND ONE SEEMS REALLY SCARY...
RRR
RRR
TNK
HE HAD SOME KIND OF...COLD BRUTAL ENERGY.
YOU NEVER KNOW WHAT A GUY LIKE THAT WILL DO!
RRR
RRR
RRR
RMBL
RRRR
RRR

HEH HEH.
ONE DOWN...
TNK
NH...
NNH ...
BBNP
TSUKUNE ...!
TNK
UHH ...
GRAB

YOU... MORON!
WHY DID YOU DO THAT?!
YOUR BODY CAN'T TAKE ANY MORE!!
AND I CAN'T HEAL YOU WITH MY BLOOD AGAIN!!
GRIP
GH...
DID YOU THINK YOU WERE SAVING ME?!
DO YOU ACTUALLY THINK I NEED HELP FROM YOU?!
GRRR
...FROM... ME...?
YOU CAN'T EVEN PROTECT YOURSELF!
DON'T EVER DO THAT AGAIN!
TMP
...

HEH... WHAT'S THE MATTER, VAMPIRE?
TMP
YOU MAKE IT SOUND LIKE IT'S TSUKUNE WHO'S THE DEAD WEIGHT.
TMM

!
BUT... MOKA...!

DON'T MOVE UNTIL I COME BACK!
I WANT TO GET YOU BACK TO THE HUMAN WORLD ALIVE.

WHAT A LOSER.
HMF. AND I WAS SO LOOKING FORWARD TO FIGHTING HIM.

JUST WAIT HERE, OKAY?!
AFTER I TAKE CARE OF THIS IDIOT...
I'LL GET YOU OUT OF HERE AND FIX YOU UP.

TOOOOM
ISN'T THAT TRUE?
IF THAT FOOL HADN'T JUMPED IN, YOU WOULD HAVE EASILY DODGED MY ATTACK.
GASP
PLIP
!!
TWIK
...IS IMPRESSIVE.
YOUR POWER ...
I DON'T HAVE TIME TO PLAY AROUND WITH A MONSTREL.
I'VE GOT NEWS FOR YOU—THIS IS GOING TO END REALLY QUICKLY.
VSH
GOR
DRIP

SO, MOKA AKASHIYA...
...YOU'RE THE VAMPIRE.
SNEER
WHAT IS TSUKUNE TO YOU?
SOME KIND OF MAGICAL FAMILIAR?
YOU SURE GOT STUCK WITH A LAME ONE.
HA
IF I WERE YOU, I'D KEEP HIM IN A CAGE!
HA
HA
HA
...
HA...?
SHUT... UP.
HA
HA
HA
HA
HA
HA
FNN
...

WOK
HUH ?!
SHE'S SO FAST!
ARRH
AND NOW I WILL--
I DON'T GIVE A DAMN ABOUT YOU.
?!!!

BAM
WTK
TAKING HOSTAGES, ATTACKING FROM BEHIND...
TOOM
YOU'RE JUST A CUR WHO CAN'T WIN WITHOUT CHEATING.
NNK
YOU'RE NOT EVEN WORTHY OF MY ANGER.
WHRL
WMP
YOU'RE JUST IN THE WAY.

I THOUGHT THE FIRST TIME WAS JUST A FLUKE, BUT...
...SHE TOOK HIM DOWN AGAIN!
...REALLY... STRONG!
SHE'S ...
HOO

THAT'S NOT FOR US TO DECIDE!
...W-WILL IT ACTUALLY WORK?!
BUT...
HF
HF
HF
HF
I GUESS... ALL WE'VE GOT LEFT NOW IS... THAT.
...RGH.

SSSSS!
HUH? WHAT'S THAT...?

MOKA...
TP...
TSUKUNE... CAN YOU STAND? WE'RE GOING HOME.

NNH...

EVERY ONE OF YOUR BLOWS HITS AS HARD AS ANYONE ELSE'S SPECIAL ATTACK.
A SIMPLE, BUT HORRIFIC TALENT...
YOU CAN CHANNEL YOUR MONSTROUS ENERGY INTO PURE POWER.
CHK
TK
HEH. SO IT'S TRUE WHAT THEY SAY ABOUT VAMPIRES...
KRAK
!

WHAT ARE YOU--
TNK
?!
THAT'S STILL NOT ENOUGH TO DEFEAT ME.
WELL ...
TNK
KLNK
!

DON'T TELL ME...
THAT SOUND ...
SS HHHH
SSSSS
SSS
SSSSS
CRAD
CRAD
CROSSES. SILVER BULLETS. OH YEAH, I'VE DONE MY RESEARCH.
VAMPIRES AREN'T JUST KNOWN FOR HAVING THE MOST STRENGTHS... THEY HAVE THE MOST WEAKNESSES TOO.

...HELPLESS AGAINST... THIS?
IS IT TRUE, MOKA? IS A VAMPIRE ...
...THAT SAPS A VAMPIRE OF ALL ITS POWER.
AND THERE IS ONE THING...

SSHHH

IS THAT...
...JUST WATER?!

AAAAA!
SHHHHH
...
NH...
GULP

WHAT DO YOU THINK OF MY SHOWER?
SHHH
SSSS
THAT TIME AT THE POOL...! WHEN VAMPIRES TOUCH WATER...
...IT'S LIKE AN ELECTRIC SHOCK!
M...
MOKA!
WMP
TLLT
TLLT
TLLT
HEH.
VVV
KH...
WOBBLE
LL
...
LLL
...BY REROUTING THE FIRE HYDRANT!
I MADE IT ESPECIALLY FOR YOU...
SSHHHH

SHUK
GUH.
!!!
UHH...
SPRT
DRIP
WATER ...
...STOLE MY POWER...
I CAN'T FIGHT BACK!

TM
MOKA!
HAHAHA! WHAT'S THE MATTER?
NOT SO ARROGANT NOW, ARE YOU?
DRIP
SSS
I...
...CAN'T ...
SHHH
HOW MANY TIMES...DO I HAVE TO TELL YOU?!
!!
B-BUT...
GULP
DON'T COME ANY CLOSER!
LEAST OF ALL FROM YOU.
I DON'T NEED HELP...
I'M NOT THE SAPPY MOKA YOU LOVE.

YOU'RE DUMBER THAN I THOUGHT.
TMP
AFTER WHAT I JUST DID TO YOU...
...YOU STILL WANT TO TAKE ME ON?!
VSSSH
TOOM
!!
OH!
PURE-BRED "PRIDE."
WHAT A LOAD OF CRAP.
HENH
THAT'S WHY YOU'RE ALL GOING TO DIE!
BAMP BAMP
IT MAKES NO DIFFER-ENCE HOW YOU FIGHT...
DOOM
RRRRMBL
NOTHING MATTERS BUT WINNING!!
RRRRMMMM
DOOM
MMM
VWSSSHHHHHHH

SHAAAK
SSSS

...THE... HELL...?
WH-WHAT ...
TNG
?!!
...!
SS
...
SS
NNNG
NNNN

KRAK
POK
KSH KSH
KKKK
KKK
M...
MOKA...
BWIK
TSUKUNE!
WMP
CHKK
VSH
AH!
...I...
N-NO WAY!
!!
HE BLOCKED IT...MY FULL-ON ATTACK!!
OH!
HIS SHOULDER—SHATTERED!
DRIP
STUPID!
WHY DID YOU DO IT?!
DRIP
DRIP
I TOLD YOU I DON'T NEED ANY HELP!
WHY ...?!

...
NO...
THE POWER... TO PROTECT YOU.
GIVE IT TO ME...
MOKA...
...GIVE ME...YOUR BLOOD.
SHHHHH
I TOLD YOU! IT'S TOO DANGEROUS!
THAT'S MAD-NESS!
...IT COULD KILL YOU!
IF I GIVE YOU MY BLOOD NOW...
WHEN YOU TOLD ME YOU DIDN'T NEED ME.
I... COULDN'T TAKE IT...
WHAT ...?
GUH ...
YOU. NOT JUST...THE OUTER MOKA.
YOU MEAN... TOO MUCH TO ME.

BECAUSE I DON'T WANT YOU TO DIE!
.....
HE'S LOSING TOO MUCH BLOOD...AND HIS TEMPERATURE'S DROPPING...
TSU-KUNE!
BRR
WHY I TOLD YOU I DIDN'T NEED YOU?
!
GRIP
NOW DO YOU UNDER-STAND...?
AND TRIED TO SEND YOU BACK TO THE HUMAN WORLD ?
WHY I PUSHED YOU AWAY?

BDMP
BDMP
BDMP
TSUKUNE ...
?!
...
...IT'S... TOO LATE...
IT'S... NO USE... HE'S NOT GETTING BETTER...
SLAP
WOBBLE
KLANK

WMP
TS... TSUKUNE ...?
!
TMP

SHHHH
SHHHH

EH...?
TSUKUNE ?

HUH...?
TWK

...ABOUT HIS ENERGY...
THERE'S SOMETHING... DIFFERENT...

I APPRECIATE THE ENTERTAIN-MENT.
...BUT I WANT YOU TO KNOW...

...
TMP
HEH HEH... WHAT NOW?
I DON'T KNOW WHAT YOU'RE THINKING ...

...TO BEAT YOU DOWN.
BWK
I WON'T EVEN NEED ANY TRICKS...
BWK WK

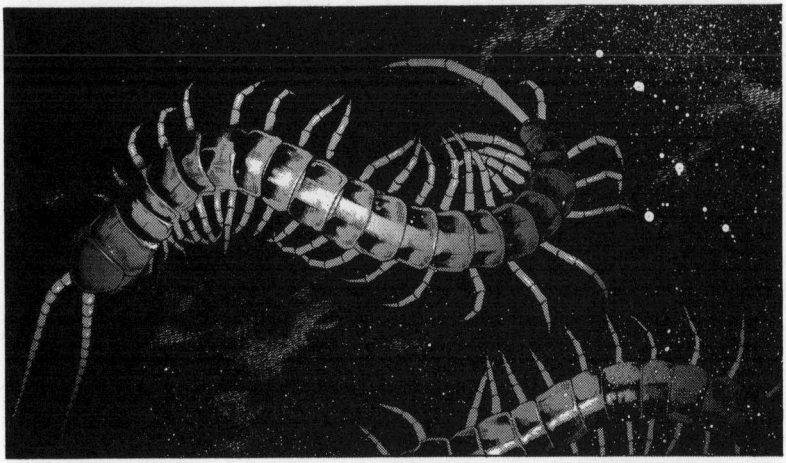

23 : Ghoul

TMP
TMP
TMP
TMP
TMP
TMP
THAT'S WHERE TSUKUNE IS BEING HELD!
I SEE IT!
!
PLEASE BE ALL RIGHT ...!
TSU-KUNE ...
RR
LBMR
HF
HF

PLUP
GH
RRR
RRR
SPURT
NH NH
SHUDDER
OO
BLP BLP
SHHHHHH
NHH.
HO O OOOO
!

23 : Ghoul

SHHHHH
HHHHHH
HHHHHH
BOMP
OH ...

HUF
HUF
DZZT

IT... WORKED?
BUT...WHY ISN'T HIS BODY SUFFERING FROM THE EFFECTS OF MY BLOOD...?
IT SHOULDN'T HAVE GONE THIS EASILY...

A VAMPIRE WHO DOESN'T MIND WATER, EH?
DON'T KNOW IF THAT MEANS YOU'RE WEAK...OR STRONG, PAL.

SH
HHHH

!
TSU-KUNE ...?
IT...IT CAN'T BE...!

HEH HEH...
TMP
!

BUT YOU'RE ENTER-TAINING— THAT'S FOR SURE!
MWK
GOOOOOOOG
MAKES ME WANT TO BEAT YOU DOWN EVEN MORE!

MIDO!

AND IF I KILL YOU...
...THEN THE PUREBREDS WILL KNOW...

HSSS
THEY'LL SEE THE TRUE POWER...
...OF THE MONSTRELS !!

HAHAHA! CHEW ON THIS, TSUKUNE AONO!
SSH
NO!!! DON'T ATTACK HIM NOW!!
TSU-KUNE IS...
SS
SSH

Fp
GWUH
?!!

DM
KKK
POP POP
KRAKK
SNAP

VSHH
TSUKUNE ...
BOOM
MMM
WHAT'S HAPPENING...?
NGH ...
GAH ...
WHAT...?
PLISH-PLISH PLISH
PLIP
PLIP

DOOM
HOOOO
TNK

!
TSUKUNE!

ARE YOU ALL RIGHT?! AND WHAT'S WITH THE WATER COMING DOWN...?!
MOKA— WHAT'S GOING ON? IS HE OKAY?!
TMP TMP TMP TMP
!
KURUMU ...?
FUSTER FUSTER
I'LL SHUT OFF THE W-W-WATER!

MY WORST FEAR COME TRUE...
WHAT ?
THIS IS A NIGHT-MARE...

...

?!!
BOOM
GASP

...
HEH...
WUK
DMM
HA HA...
WAK
HA HA HA HA HA HA!
WUK
KRAK
WUK
THD
WUK
WUK
WUK
?
WUK
?!
TS-TSUKUNE ?
WHAT ARE YOU...?
WK
WK
WK
WK

WHACK
MIDO'S UNCONSCIOUS!
HE'S GONNA KILL HIM!!
KSH
GAAA! SOMEBODY STOP HIM!
TWTCH TWTCH

YAAAAA
WUP
DM
DM
KRAK
WUK
BRRRR
I-IT CAN'T BE...
...PLEASE TELL ME... THAT ISN'T...
...TSUKUNE?

Bite-Size Encyclopedia

Ghoul

Created when an evil spirit possesses a corpse. Favorite food: human meat. Feeds on children and cadavers exhumed from graves.
Weakness: the divine and spiritual. They avoid religious symbols.

READ THIS WAY
TSUKUNE ...
...A GHOUL ...?
FIRE
Rrrg!
Rrrg!
KUK
FIRE
PLIP
PLIP
PLIP
PLIP

PLIP
PLIP
TP
PLIP
PLIP
PLIP
PLIP

?!!
TP...
MOKA? WHAT ARE YOU...?
WAIT!

ドゴッ

FORGIVE ME...
TP
Ngh...
Ggak...
I CAN'T SAVE YOU NOW.
SPURT
THIS IS THE ONLY WAY.
PLEASE DON'T HATE ME, TSUKUNE...

KRAKK
KK

KRAK
KK
KZZT
KK

THE POOR LAD...
...HAS DESCENDED INTO GHOULDOM.

KZZT
THIS ENERGY!
...
YES...

HE IS TO BE PITIED... FOR HE CAN NEVER BE WHAT HE ONCE WAS.
CURSED TO WANDER FOREVER IN SEARCH OF BLOOD.
SURELY DEATH IS BETTER THAN THIS.
HWO OOO OOO

AND IT SEEMS THE GIRL...
...UNDER-STANDS THAT ALL TOO WELL...
THOK
TMM
WK
WUP
KO
K
...KH!
TM
TM
TM
NKH...
DM
M

I CAN MOVE NOW THAT THE WATER HAS STOPPED, BUT...IT DAMAGED ME.
TMP
SMP
I'VE LOST TOO MUCH BLOOD... SO LITTLE STRENGTH ...
OH...
SHIIIIIIII
TINK
TINK
...WHO'S GOING TO GET KILLED...IF I CAN'T DO THIS QUICKLY...
TSUKUNE WASN'T HURT AT ALL...I'M THE ONE...
STOP!
WHAT ARE YOU DOING, MOKA?! BE CAREFUL OR YOU'LL KILL TSUKUNE!
NO—THE TRUTH IS... HE'S ALREADY DEAD.
?!!
WHAT ...?
I'M GOING TO KILL HIM.
THAT'S RIGHT.

I'M ONLY SORRY THAT HE WASN'T BLESSED WITH THE BETTER FATE—
—TRUE DEATH.
INSTEAD OF THE UNDEAD LIFE OF A GHOUL.

HE HAS NOTHING LIKE A LIFE NOW. NO SOUL, NO WILL.
HE LIVES ONLY TO SERVE HIS INSTINCTIVE LUST FOR BLOOD AND FLESH.
IF WE LEAVE HIM BE, HE'LL BE KILLING HUMANS SOON.

YOU KNOW THAT TSUKUNE WOULD NEVER HAVE WANTED THAT.
AND THE ONE TO BLAME FOR MAKING HIM INTO THIS...IS ME.
HMP

?!!
NO!!
WSH
TMP
YOUR HANDS ARE SHAKING!
DON'T ACT ALL TOUGH WITH ME, MOKA!
!
STEP ASIDE. NOW.
DO YOU VALUE YOUR LIFE, KURUMU ?
...

GLP
STILL...
GLP
I KNOW HOW MUCH YOU CARE.
YOU TRY TO MAKE US THINK YOU'RE A COLD FISH...THAT YOU DON'T HAVE ANY FEELINGS... BUT I KNOW...
I SEE RIGHT THROUGH YOU...
...WITHOUT GOING THROUGH US!!!!
I CAN'T LET YOU DO THIS, MOKA. YOU CAN'T HURT HIM...
YOU ...
!

HWP
HUH ...?
I TOLD YOU TO GET OUT OF MY WAY!
...FOOL !!
VS
SH
TM

SPURT

TS...
...TSU-KUNE?
SHP
LICK
LICK
LICK
LICK
KILL
LICK
!
KILL
GLP

HE HE HE HE HE HE HE HE HE HE
KILL! KILL!
KILL! KILL!
FWAP
FWAP
FWAP
FWAPPA
FWAPPA

TSUKUNE!
WAM

GNUH!
WNCH
SPURT
GNARH!
BLRRRRK
WHUD
KRAK KRAK
KRAK
NNF!
WHUK
...
KK
HWP KRAK
DMM
HWP

K-KURUMU! HANG ON!
YOU'RE HURT, BUT—
DRIP DRIP
S...
...S... SAVE...
!!
RRRRR
Hee Hee

NOT ME!!
I'LL LIVE!! JUST SAVE...
...TSUKUNE!!
!

PLEASE...
...SAVE HIM...
SOB

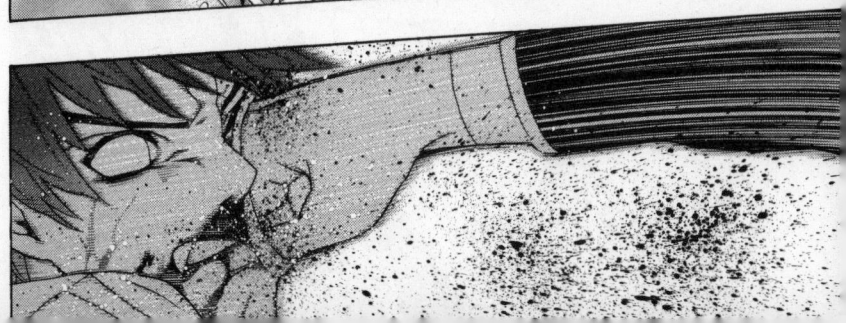

I WOULDN'T LET YOU GO NO MATTER WHAT... BUT...
IF THIS WERE JUST ABOUT ME...
TSU-KUNE...
CAN DEATH BE A CRUELER FATE THAN LIFE WITHOUT A SOUL?
KILLING PEOPLE... EVEN YOUR FRIENDS...
YOU'RE THE ONE WHO WOULD SUFFER.
I'M SO SORRY...
I DREAMED OF SO MUCH MORE FOR US...

TSUKUNE!

VSSS
SHH
FNNN
WSH

?!!
!!!!
?!!
RRR
VWISH
RR
RR RRR
RMBL
TP
TP
HEE
VIP
!
TMP
HOW DARE YOU GET IN MY WAY?!
WHO DO YOU THINK YOU ARE?!
?!!
TNG
TNG

HONESTLY... AND AFTER ALL THE TROUBLE I WENT THROUGH TO GET HERE!
TNG
GRIP
SHOW SOME APPRECIATION, MOKA AKASHIYA.
?!!
WAIT... WHAT ARE YOU GOING TO DO TO TSUKUNE?
TINK
GASP
A CROSS ?!
Amen

BOOM

SS
S SS
SS
GLEAM
TUG
HEE
WH-WHO ARE YOU...?
TM
!
WSSH
THOSE MARKS... THEY'RE DISAPPEARING?!
?!
VISH
!!!
AND HE'S HERE TO SAVE TSUKUNE.
HE'S AN EXORCIST.
VOOSH
VISH
DON'T WORRY... WE'RE NOT THE ENEMY.

RUBY!!!
LONG TIME NO SEE, EVERYBODY.
I'VE COME TO REPAY THE FAVOR I OWE YOU FROM WITCH'S KNOLL.

ROSARIO+VAMPIRE

I WISH YOU HAD NEVER COME TO OUR MONSTER WORLD.
I'M SORRY. NONE OF THIS IS YOUR FAULT.
...TSU-KUNE.
GOOD-BYE...

24 : Nightmare

JUST A DREAM...

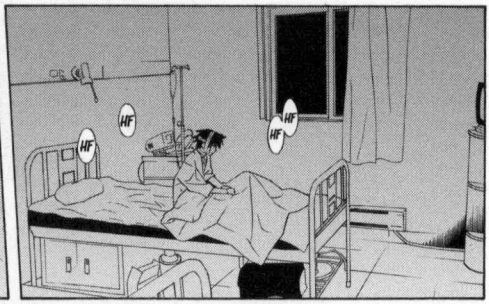

A DREAM ABOUT MOKA...
STABBING ME IN THE HEART!

YOU'RE AWAKE, TSUKUNE...?

FLIT FLIT

GLINT
AAAA!!
H-HEY!! WHERE AM I?!!
GASP!
EEP!
WHO ARE YOU?!
AND HOW DID YOU KNOW?!
OW...
THROB
THROB
THROB
BUT WHO ARE YOU?!
...
EVER SINCE YOUR GIRLFRIEND NEARLY DID YOU IN.
YOU'VE BEEN UNCONSCIOUS.
YOU SHOULDN'T GET TOO WORKED UP...
SHH...
?!!

Y-YOU'RE ...
HUH ...?
YOU'RE WITH FRIENDS NOW.
TMP
HE'S JUST AN EXORCIST. HE SAVED YOU.
DON'T WORRY...
TMMP
...RUBY ?!!
?
YOU'VE BEEN ASLEEP FOR FOUR DAYS!
AGH?!! KURUMU?
KRAK
POP
SK
WEEEEZ
TSUKUNE! YOU'RE BACK!

IT'S GOOD TO SEE YOU AGAIN.
AND GOOD TO BE ABLE TO REPAY YOU, TOO.

HSH...

...?
WAA
WAA WAA
WH-WHAT'S GOING ON...?
PAT PAT

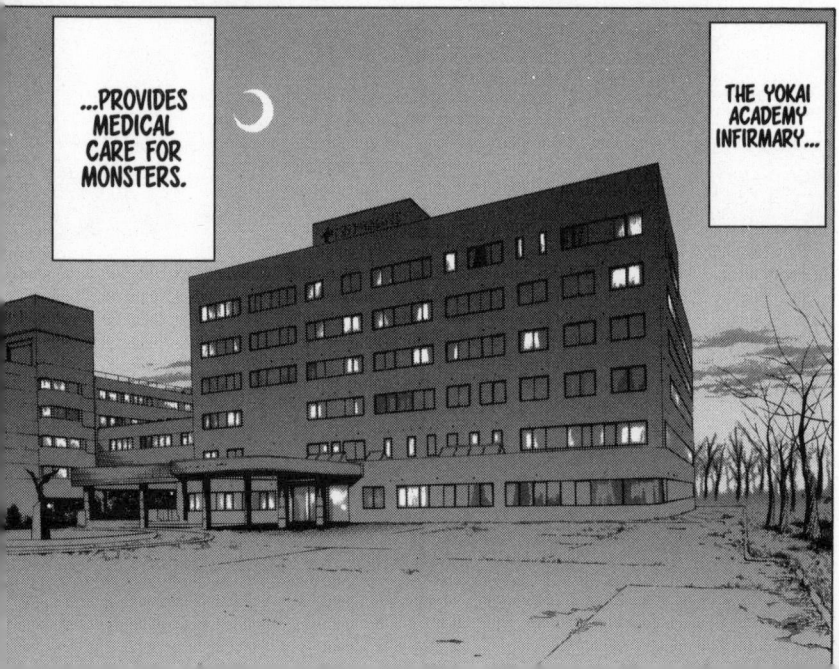
THE YOKAI ACADEMY INFIRMARY...
...PROVIDES MEDICAL CARE FOR MONSTERS.

404
Aono
WHOA, WHOA, WHOA!
YOU MEAN MOKA REALLY WAS GONNA KILL ME?!
BECAUSE I WAS TURNING INTO SOME KIND OF... GHOUL?!

LOOK AT YOUR RIGHT HAND, TSUKUNE.
!
KLINK

IT WAS AWFUL! SHE WASN'T PULLING HER PUNCHES AT ALL!
FLAP FLAP
AND YOU WERE HARDLY ANY Bbetter! LIKE SOME KIND OF PSYCHO KILLER!
PLEASE TELL ME YOU'RE MAKING THIS UP!
BRRR

WHAT ...?
THE HOLY LOCK...
...WORKS ON THE SAME PRINCIPLE AS MOKA'S ROSARIO SEAL.
IT LOCKS DOWN THE VAMPIRE BLOOD IN YOUR BODY...

IT'S THE ONLY THING PREVENTING YOU FROM TURNING INTO A GHOUL.
IF IT EVER COMES OFF... YOU'RE DOOMED.

JUST DOING A FAVOR FOR...AN OLD FRIEND.
A FRIEND ?
YES...

UH ...
THANKS. SERIOUSLY. BUT...
WHY DID YOU SAVE ME?
GULP

THE BUS DRIVER?!!
HIM.
WHAT?
GONNNNNG!

HOW DOES HE KNOW THESE THINGS?!
?!
HEH HEH
...SAID YOU WERE IN TERRIBLE DANGER!
HE CAME TO US...

KLINK

HEE
YADA YADA
ANYWAY... BE CAREFUL, SON!

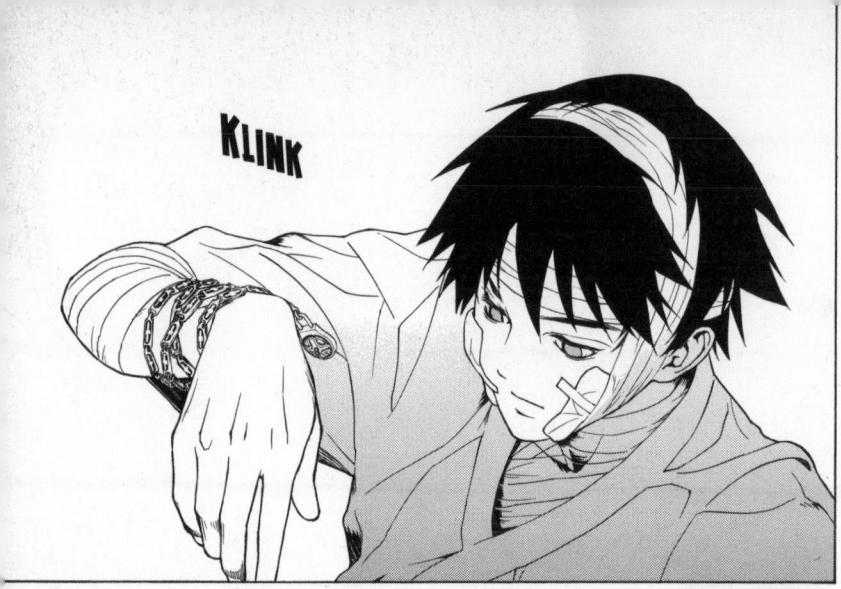
KLINK

?
!!
HEY...! WHERE'S MOKA?!
VIP
VIP

'CAUSE... SHE'S THE ONE WHO HURT YOU...
...NOT HERE.
SHE'S ...

SHE JUST CAN'T FACE YOU.
GLEEM
TINK

HEY...
KIIIN
!
GLEEM
HOW LONG ARE YOU GONNA STAND OUT HERE?
WE HAVE TO GO!

BECAUSE OF WHO WE VAMPIRES ARE...AT OUR CORE.

I ALMOST TURNED TSUKUNE INTO A GHOUL.
AND I AL-MOST KILLED HIM.
IF YOU TRY TO BE WITH HIM LIKE BEFORE, THEN... IT'S BOUND TO HAPPEN AGAIN.
KIIIN

WE NEVER ...
...SHOULD HAVE GOTTEN SO CLOSE TO HIM.

!

HE GOT SAVED THIS TIME. NEXT TIME, HE MIGHT NOT BE SO LUCKY...

SHOOP
...
MOKA...?

...
I GUESS IT WAS JUST MY IMAGINATION...

!!
TSU-KUNE...

KLIK

SHOOP

KLIK
KLIK
KLIK

I HEAR...
...HE'S STILL ALIVE. AND CONSCIOUS NOW.
THE PUNK WHO HUMILIATED YOU...

SORRY, PAL. ♡

SHUK

TO CLEAN UP YOUR BIG...
...MESS.
N... NO...
SKWK
SKWK
SKWK
WHY DO YOU THINK THEY SENT IN THE "CLEANER"?
HMM?
GKK...

YOU'VE TURNED OUT TO BE WORTH-LESS.
ALL OF US AT THE TOP ARE DIS-APPOINTED...
SKWK
SKWK
SKWK
YOU KNOW HOW WE MONSTRELS ARE. WE DON'T FORGIVE LOSERS.

FFD

SPLURRRT
GAAAAH!

TO MAKE IT WORTH MY WHILE... I'LL HAVE TO BE ESPECIALLY CRUEL.
LJK
NOW I'M GOING TO HAVE TO KILL AONO MYSELF.

HELLO!
I'LL BE TAKING OFF YOUR BANDAGES.
Nurse Trainee
Mako Yakumaru

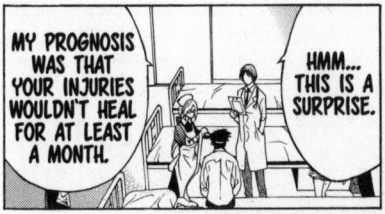
HMM... THIS IS A SURPRISE.
MY PROGNOSIS WAS THAT YOUR INJURIES WOULDN'T HEAL FOR AT LEAST A MONTH.

SHWR

I DON'T KNOW WHAT TO SAY, EXCEPT... CONGRATULATIONS!
YOU'LL BE CHECKING OUT SOON, MR. AONO.
Doctor Yutaka Yuji
YAY!
YOU DON'T WANT TO LAND RIGHT BACK HERE AGAIN, DO YOU?
...
THERE ARE A LOT OF THEM... AND YOU NEVER KNOW WHERE THEY MIGHT BE HIDING.
YOU BETTER WATCH YOUR BACK...
!
SCRATCH SCRATCH
HEY...I HEAR YOU'VE BEEN GETTING INTO SPATS WITH THE MONSTRELS.

I'LL PROTECT HIM FROM NOW ON! ♡
HE'LL BE FINE!
VWIP
BDMP

AWW, YOU GUYS...
HEE HEE ...
AND I'LL DO WHAT I CAN AS WELL!
I'M GONNA PROTECT HIM TOO!
RUB
RUB

KURUMU ...?
I WOULD NEVER LET ANYTHING BAD HAPPEN TO YOU!

UM... SINCE THE BEGIN-NING ...?
MIZORE?!! HOW LONG HAVE YOU BEEN HERE?!!
SO WHY DIDN'T YOU SAY SOME-THING?!
CREEPY!

...I'LL ALWAYS BE WATCHING YOU.
AND... YOU KNOW...
LICK

...
!!

I'M GLAD YOU'RE BETTER, TSUKUNE.
BLAH
BLAH
BLAH
GOOD...
YADA YADA
BLAH BLAH
...

BUT WITH SO MANY GOOD MONSTERS TO PROTECT YOU...
I THOUGHT, SINCE YOU'RE HUMAN, YOU SHOULDN'T BE IN OUR WORLD...
No way!
But isn't that...?
Aha ha ha...
What?
AND I'M GLAD YOU HAVE SO MANY FRIENDS.

...YOU'LL BE SAFE.

WITHOUT ME...
...YOU'LL BE SAFE.

SLOOP
MOKA?
I KNEW IT!!!
SOMEHOW I COULD... SENSE YOUR PRESENCE!
Amazing!
I WAS AFRAID YOU WEREN'T GOING TO COME!
BUT NOW THAT YOU'RE HERE... EVERY-THING'S ALL RIGHT!
!!
BLUSH
OH...

READ THIS WAY
TSUKUNE ...
...
UM...
MAY I HAVE A FEW MOMENTS OF YOUR TIME, DOCTOR?
MISS MAKO..?
GIGGLE
OH, HOW I WISH I HAD SUCH CLOSE FRIENDS!
ISN'T IT HEART-WARMING, DOCTOR?
I'D JUST LIKE TO...
...DISCUSS SOMETHING WITH YOU...IN PRIVATE.

...
POP

MOKA...
COME BACK INTO THE ROOM WITH ME.
...

MOKA?
...?

SHAKE
SHAKE

TSUKUNE... I...
I REMEMBER WHAT HAPPENED WHEN MY ROSARIO WAS OFF.
IT'S A LITTLE HAZY, BUT...I HAVE SOME MEMORIES OF WHEN I'M THE "INNER ME" AND...

I'LL NEVER BE ABLE TO FORGET IT! THE MEMORY IS STORED IN MY BODY FOREVER!
WHAT I FELT...
...YOUR BONES SNAP-PING...THE SOUND OF YOUR SCREAMS ...
...HIT YOU... WHEN I... WAS TRYING TO KILL YOU...
I CAN'T FORGET WHEN I...
TIMBE TIMBE
JOLT
I COULDN'T BEAR THAT, TSUKUNE.
AND I THINK...IF I STAY WITH YOU...I'LL END UP HURTING YOU AGAIN.
MOKA...
I'M SORRY... I'M SO SORRY.

I'M SORRY...
THAT'S WHY...
I CAN'T BE WITH YOU ANYMORE.

DASH
TM
TM
TM
!!
TS-TSUKUNE !!

TMP
TP
TP
TP

SO YOU'RE MOKA AKASHIYA ...
BE CAREFUL! A PACK OF MONSTRELS HAS TARGETED YOU!

OH—!
DMM
E-EXCUSE ME...
...

ARE YOU ALL RIGHT, MOKA?

ARE YOU CRYING?
DOC-TOR...
HOW...?

SHF
YOU'RE BEING AWFULLY CARELESS.
YOU'RE A MARKED PERSON.
YOU SHOULD SURROUND YOURSELF WITH DEFENSES... AND FRIENDS!
HOW DO YOU KNOW ABOUT THAT?
I MEAN, I JUST FOUND OUT MYSELF...
KLK
PWF
BUT...
TH...THANK YOU...
D... DOCTOR ...?
HOW DO I KNOW...
YES, YES. AWFULLY CARELESS ...
TAK

AAAAA!!
OOO
M
...BECAUSE I'M THE ONE WHO IS AFTER YOU!
?!!
KRAK
CRAK
OF COURSE I KNOW...
...YOU ASK?!
HSSSS
BLP
BLP
PLEASE... I DON'T UNDER-STAND...
?! DOCTOR...

HEH...
BLP
BLP
BLP
I TOLD YOU TO KEEP YOUR FRIENDS AROUND YOU!
LICK

NO MATTER WHAT YOU SAY, MOKA...

FWIP
TSU-KUNE... WHERE ARE YOU GOING?
YOU'RE NOT THINKING OF GOING AFTER MOKA...?

...
TP

SORRY...
!!
BUT I CAN'T JUST LET YOU WALK AWAY.

HWK
KK
KK
KK
NNH...
!!
VVP
TIME FOR YOUR INJECTION! HOLD STILL!
SPT
THIS WILL MAKE YOU VERY HAPPY.
SO HAPPY THAT YOU'LL DO WHATEVER I SAY.
LIKE A GOOD LITTLE PUPPET!
NO!

D-DON'T... PLEASE LET ME GO!
WHY DO YOU WANT TO HURT US?!
WE DON'T WANT TO FIGHT ANYONE!

AFTER YOU, IT'LL BE TSUKUNE'S TURN. GIGGLE!
NN N
TWK
TWK
TWK
AND WITH YOUR HELP I CAN DO IT...
...WITHOUT LEAVING A TRACE.

NO! I CAN'T LET HIM!
PAP
PAP
GOT TO DO SOME-THING...

TUP
...SOME-HOW...
...I'VE GOT TO...

AND WHAT COULD POSSIBLY BE CRUELER...?
GIGGLE
BRR

KSSSHH
...SAVE TSUKUNE !!
HF
HF
HF
HF
HF
WMMMMMPP
!!
...
GUH.
KS
SSH
DRIP

!!
SHOOP
DOCTOR ...?! IS SOMETHING THE MATTER?
I THOUGHT I HEARD A...
NURSE!!
THE DOCTOR ATTACKED ME!
HE WAS GOING TO INJECT ME WITH SOME WEIRD DRUG!
VSH
OH...
PLEASE!! HELP ME!!
SHP
!?
GASP
W-WHAT ?
THAT WON'T DO. NOT AT ALL.
OH MY...
PWK
PIP

YOU MEAN YOU...
POKE
...HAVEN'T GOTTEN...
...YOUR SHOT YET?!

N-NO...
BAD LITTLE GIRL. YOU SHOULD FOLLOW DOCTOR'S ORDERS!
WELL, I GUESS THERE'S NO HELP FOR IT.
SEE MY FINGER ...? ♡
WH...
WHAT ...?!
SWKK
SWKK

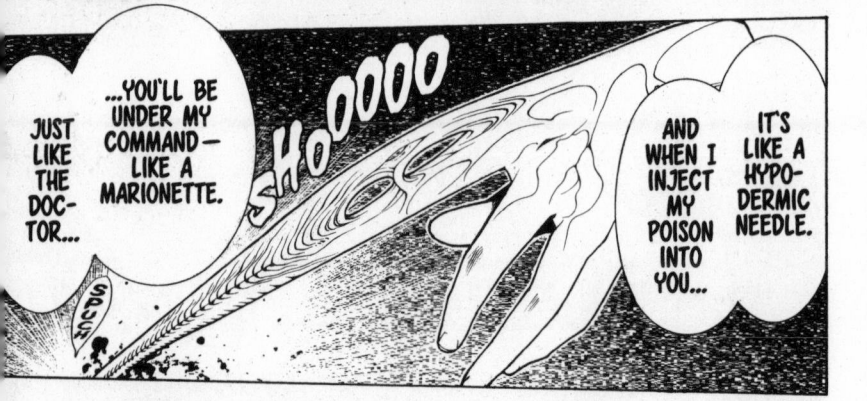
IT'S LIKE A HYPO-DERMIC NEEDLE.
AND WHEN I INJECT MY POISON INTO YOU...
...YOU'LL BE UNDER MY COMMAND— LIKE A MARIONETTE.
JUST LIKE THE DOC-TOR...
SHOOOOO
SDJJH

!!
WOULDN'T WANT YOU THINKING THAT FOOL'S A MONSTREL.
!!
Y-YOU MEAN...
YOU FORCED HIM TO ATTACK ME?!
TREMBLE TREMBLE

THEN... THAT MEANS THAT YOU...
KSH
YOU'RE A MONSTREL ?!
KLAK
WSSSH

GLEAM

SO CLEVER!
BUT NOW IT'S YOUR TURN TO BE MY MARIONETTE...
...MOKA AKASHIYA.

KRRRAK
MMBBBL
RRRPRRM
TSU...KU... NE...
VWIP VWIP
MOKA ...?
DID SHE GO HOME ALREADY ...?
TP TP

Ghoul [The End]

ROSARIO + VAMPIRE

End-of-Volume Theater

VI

The Answer Is...♡

Tell Us ♡, Teacher!

A Girl's Heart

The Truth Behind The Three Sizes

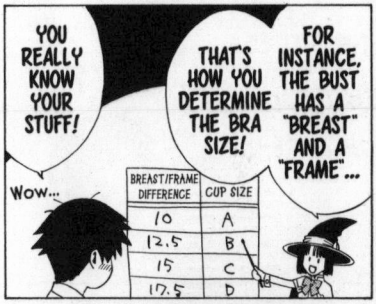

BREAST/FRAME DIFFERENCE	CUP SIZE
10	A
12.5	B
15	C
17.5	D

Please send questions and fan letters to ➡ Rosario+Vampire Fan Mail, VIZ Media, P.O. Box 77084, San Francisco, CA 94107

Rosario & Vampire

Akihisa Ikeda

• Staff •

Makoto Saito

Takafumi Okubo

• Help •

Kenji Tashiro

Yuichiro Higuchi

• CG •

Takaharu Yoshizawa

Akihisa Ikeda

• Editing •

Satoshi Adachi

• Comic •

Kenju Noro

Crypt Sheet for Volume 7: Shikigami

QUIZ 7

AS A HUMAN ATTENDING A SCHOOL FOR MONSTERS, ENCOUNTERING AN EXORCIST MIGHT EXPEL...

a. the demon inside you

b. you from school

c. a big burp

NORA
THE LAST CHRONICLE OF DEVILDOM
By Kazunari Kakei
An Exchange Student From Hell...
LITERALLY!
SHONEN JUMP ADVANCED
1
Story & Art by
Kazunari Kakei
NORA
THE LAST CHRONICLE OF DEVILDOM
MANGA SERIES ON SALE NOW
SHONEN JUMP
THE WORLD'S MOST POPULAR MANGA
On sale at www.shonenjump.com
Also available at your local bookstore and comic store.
NORA - THE LAST CHRONICLE OF THE DEVILDOM
© 2004 by Kazunari Kakei/SHUEISHA Inc.
RATED T FOR OLDER TEEN
ratings.viz.com
viz media
www.viz.com

黒姫
KUROHIME
SJ ADVANCED
CURSE OF THE WITCH GUNSLINGER
$7.99
Manga series on sale now!
SHONEN JUMP ADVANCED
On sale at:
www.shonenjump.com
Also available at your local bookstore and comic store.
RATED T+ FOR OLDER TEEN ratings.viz.com
viz media
MAHO-TSUKAI KUROHIME © 2000 by Masanori • Ookamigumi • Katakura/SHUEISHA Inc.

SJ ADVANCED
Can teenage exorcist Allen Walker defeat the Millennium Earl...and save the world?
Manga on sale now!
D.GRAY-MAN
Katsura Hoshino
1
D.Gray-Man
SHONEN JUMP ADVANCED
Story & Art by KATSURA HOSHINO
D.Gray-Man™
$7.99
SHONEN JUMP ADVANCED
On sale at:
www.shonenjump.com
Also available at your local bookstore and comic store
RATED T+ FOR OLDER TEEN
viz media

Is Gin the best hope of the samurai,
or their worst nightmare?
SJ ADVANCED
$7.99
GIN TAMA
1
SHONEN JUMP ADVANCED
HIDEAKI SORACHI
MANGA ON SALE NOW!
GIN TAMA
SHONEN JUMP ADVANCED
On sale at:
www.shonenjump.com
Also available at your local bookstore and comic store.
RATED T
TEEN
ratings.viz.com
viz media
www.viz.com

BEHIND THE SHADOWS

SJ ADVANCED

RalΩGrad

From the artist of
Death Note

Manga series on sale now!

Story by **TSUNEO TAKANO**
Art by **TAKESHI OBATA**

SHONEN JUMP
THE WORLD'S MOST POPULAR MANGA

On sale at: **www.shonenjump.com**
Also available at your local bookstore and comic store.

RALΩGRAD © 2006 by Tsuneo Takano, Takeshi Obata/SHUEISHA Inc.

RATED T+ FOR OLDER TEEN
ratings.viz.com

viz media
www.viz.com

ADVANCED
Reborn will make all your death wishes come true!
ONLY $7.99
Manga series on sale now!
リボーン REBORN!
リボーン REBORN!™
viz media
www.viz.com
RATED T+ FOR OLDER TEEN
ratings.viz.com
On sale at:
www.shonenjump.com
Also available at your local bookstore and comic store
SHONEN JUMP ADVANCED
KATEKYO HITMAN REBORN! © 2002 by Akira Amano/SHUEISHA Inc.

the GREATEST DETECTIVE, the GREATEST CITY... the GREATEST CHALLENGE!

SJ FICTION

DEATH NOTE

デスノート

ANOTHER NOTE: THE LOS ANGELES BB MURDER CASES

LOS ANGELES AUTHORITIES ARE TRACKING A SERIAL KILLER WHOSE CLUES ARE SO COMPLEX THAT EVEN L, THE WORLD'S MOST DECORATED DETECTIVE, CAN'T DECIPHER THEM. ENLISTING THE HELP OF FBI AGENT NAOMI MISORA, CAN L CRACK THE CASE -AND PRESERVE HIS REPUTATION- BEFORE THE VICTIMS OUTNUMBER THE CLUES?

FIND OUT IN *ANOTHER NOTE: THE LOS ANGELES BB MURDER CASES*—NOVEL IN STORES NOW

GET THE COMPLETE *DEATH NOTE* COLLECTION—BUY THE MANGA, PROFILES BOOK AND ANIME TODAY!

SHONEN JUMP ADVANCED

On sale at deathnote.viz.com

Also available at your local bookstore and comic store.

RATED T+ FOR OLDER TEEN ratings.viz.com

viz media

www.viz.com

DEATH NOTE - ANOTHER NOTE LOS ANGELES BB RENZOKU SATSUJIN JIKEN -

© 2006 by NISIO ISIN, Tsugumi Ohba, Takeshi Obata/SHUEISHA Inc.

Tell us what you think about SHONEN JUMP manga!

Our survey is now available online.
Go to: ***www.SHONENJUMP.com/mangasurvey***

Help us make our product offering better!

BLEACH © 2001 by Tite Kubo/SHUEISHA Inc. NARUTO © 1999 by Masashi Kishimoto/SHUEISHA Inc.
DEATH NOTE © 2003 by Tsugumi Ohba, Takeshi Obata/SHUEISHA Inc. ONE PIECE © 1997 by Eiichiro Oda/SHUEISHA Inc.

Full of FREE previews and tons of new manga for you to explore

From legendary manga like *Dragon Ball* to *Bakuman*., the newest series from the creators of *Death Note*, the best manga in the world is now available on the iPad through the official VIZ Manga app.

- Free App
- New content weekly
- Free chapter 1 previews

BAKUMAN.© 2008 by Tsugumi Ohba, Takeshi Obata/SHUEISHA Inc. BLEACH © 2001 by Tite Kubo/SHUEISHA Inc. NARUTO © 1999 by Masashi Kishimoto/SHUEISHA Inc.
DEATH NOTE © 2003 by Tsugumi Ohba, Takeshi Obata/SHUEISHA Inc. DRAGON BALL © 1984 by BIRD STUDIO/SHUEISHA Inc. ONE PIECE © 1997 by Eiichiro Oda/SHUEISHA Inc.

viz media
www.viz.co

SHONEN JUMP

The World's Most Popular Manga

P9-DEH-056

OFF the cover price!

270+ pages of the HOTTEST MANGA STORIES every month combined with the latest in GAMES, ANIME, TRADING CARDS, and more!

PLUS Exclusive, ULTRA-RARE PREMIUMS in almost every issue—including RED-HOT TRADING CARDS!

That's like getting 4 issues FREE!

2 EASY WAYS TO SUBSCRIBE
1 Visit www.shonenjump.com
2 Call 1-800-541-7919

10 HUGE issues for ONLY $26.95*

* Offer good whiles supplies last. Void where prohibited by law. Offer valid with full payment of SHONEN JUMP subscription. Canada price: $36.95 USD, including GST, HST, and QST. US/CAN orders only. Allow 6-8 weeks for delivery.

YU-GI-OH! 5D's © 2009 by Masahiro Hikokubo, Masashi Sato Based on Animation TV series YU-GI-OH!5D's © 1996 Kazuki Takahashi © 2008 NAS•TV TOKYO DRAGON BALL © 1984 by BIRD STUDIO/SHUEISHA Inc. NARUTO © 1999 by Masashi Kishimoto/SHUEISHA Inc.